CULTURAL AWAKENINGS

Insightful Writings

Matahari V.

H
HANSIB

Price: CAN $20.00

Proceeds from sales to go to Diya Foundation for victims of Fibrous Dysplasia of the skull

To order copies, please contact:
malavthapar@hotmail.com

First published in 2020 by Hansib Publications
P.O. Box 226, Hertford, SG14 3WY, UK

info@hansibpublications.com
www.hansibpublications.com

Copyright © Mala Thapar, 2020
malavthapar@hotmail.com

All images by Avinash Pasricha unless otherwise credited

ISBN 978-1-912662-22-7
ISBN 978-1-912662-23-4 (Kindle)
ISBN 978-1-912662-24-1 (ePub)

Mala Thapar (a.k.a. Matahari V.) has asserted her moral right to be identified as the author of this work.

All rights reserved. No part of this publication may be reproduced, stored in a retrieval system, or transmitted, in any form or by any means, electronic, mechanical, photocopying, recording or otherwise, without the prior permission of the author.

Printed in Great Britain

for
Philip Pinto, my mentor
and
Brian Beal, my motivator

FOREWORD

Ours is a troubled world. Of all life forms on earth, only we humans can plant and harvest crops, write poetry and compose opera, become partners in our own evolution. And yet we also hunt and persecute each other. It seems that our world is a very busy place and our state of life bordering on the frenetic. We hardly have time for meaningful relationships or generative conversations. So many families go through the motions of supporting and caring for one another and end up stressed by the individualism and pressure that is thrust on them by social media.

"And yet, this same wondrous species of ours now seems bent on putting an end not only to its own evolution but to that of most life on our globe, threatening our planet with ecological catastrophe or nuclear annihilation."[1]

It appears to me that ***Cultural Awakenings is written for times like ours***. It attempts to give us the eyes to see deeper into the innerness of things, to feed our soul and to taste the beauty of life that is given to us freely – if we but stop for a while. By "soul" I do not mean that amorphous,

---

1. Excerpt From: Riane Eisler. "The Chalice and the Blade." Apple Books.

airy, invisible part that is me. I mean it is that part of me that wants more of life and meaning than I presently have. It is that part of me that lives on even when the body ages and dies. It is the real me after I have sifted through the layers of the false self.

Coming from the East, yet having lived in the West, the author brings her many varied experiences to this work. She speaks from experience and is one who has reflected on that experience. She knows that she has discovered some truly sparkling gems of wisdom over the years and is eager to share these with the reader. *"Awakening of consciousness is a flight from 'one' self to another self and to the Universe. As consciousness expands, I discover new ways of perceiving, being and becoming. I share some of my thoughts and experiences with you."*

The book is to be read slowly, chewed and digested. Take time to ponder the questions that are asked. These are the essence of what it is to be human. A look at the chapter headings is very revealing and allows us a glimpse into what is in store for us: Freedom to Explore, Thanksgiving, Aloneness, Fear and Love, and so on. Every one of them is balm for an aching soul.

Joseph Philip Pinto
C.F.C.
Rome, Italy

CONTENTS

PART ONE

Cultural Awakenings 11
Nature of the Soul 16
A Journey with His Holiness: the Dalai Lama 19
Meeting Mother Teresa 25
Meeting Van Gogh 29
Freedom to Explore 33
The Prodigal Son 35
Thanksgiving 38
Perceptions 41
Extraordinary Perceptions 43
Renaissance Period and Perceptions 46
Associations 48
Aloneness 53
Meaningful Coincidences 55
Fear and Love 58
Encounters 59
Transformational Leadership 61
Fragmentation 65
Freedom 67
Education of the Heart 69
Ass- u- me 73

PART TWO

'Brahm and Bhram'	77
Third Eye Perceptions	80
Desired Outcomes	83
Truth	85
Understanding Oneself	87
The Significance of Pause	90
Hope	92
Women's Stories	97
Mystery	100
The Landscape of Ageing	101
Relationship with Time	102
The Wisdom Tree	103
Science of Wisdom	107
The Maze	109
The Bird flies home	111
Acknowledgements	115

PART ONE

Diya

"Where is the soul?" asked the child
"I am looking at it", said the man
"Where, I don't see it?"
"It shines through your eyes"
Both smiled a knowing smile.

Cultural Awakenings

Awakening of cultural consciousness is a flight from 'one' self to another self and to the Universe. As consciousness expands, I discover new ways of perceiving, being and becoming. Cultural Awakenings is a book about the 'Soul' and its longing for manifestation. We are mystified by it, because we cannot see it. The world within us is as vast as the ocean. Yet, we are afraid to dive in.

Culture is not just outside us, but also inside us. We seldom venture here. This is because of the ego. It blocks us from soul searching.

External cultures change continuously from monogamous to heterogeneous. People move globally, carrying their minds with them, and along with it the vast field of consciousness, that waits to be tapped. Educated in different disciplines and ways, divisive and illusive in nature, the ego works at two levels: as the false self and the true self. Intermarriages and live-in partners influence life and thought. Lines blur.

There comes a turning point. Confused, because we have not developed a guide within us, we look for answers outside us. These perplex as they vary in perspective.

Can anyone really know us, if we do not know ourselves? How can we know ourselves, if we are continuously battling with the world outside us? Worried and fearful, what will happen to us if we stop, we jostle for power and position, chasing success, power, position and money. Is that what the soul really craves for? I say, 'What will happen if we stop in this race?'

Like the butterfly we will find wings, another way, another flight, another station to arrive at, without any preparation or a guidebook. We will learn along the way.

The cultural fabric is rich. Ideas abound. Somewhere deep-down, humanity realizes its interconnectedness, unity in diversity. Duality gives way to oneness. Yet, wars continue. Internet wars. Virtual wars that lead to real wars. There is fear of chemical wars, biological wars and nuclear wars, as the bit sphere takes over the biosphere. Tempers fly high.

There is one answer: *Soulful Living!*

Mindscapes: "The mind is indeed restless, Arjuna: it is indeed hard to train. But by constant practice, and by freedom from passions, the mind in truth can be trained."[1]

If everything begins and ends in the mind where is the mind?

---
1. Lord Krishna 6:35 Bhagavat Gita

The mind is instrumental in functioning, relating, responding, remembering and much more. We use only a fraction of it in our lifetime. I wonder why? Is it because we have not learnt to be mindful? Or is it because our minds are too full of irrelevant stuff? We clutter our minds, giving space to whatever comes our way. How often do we turn them inwards towards our soul to be replenished? Inundated with innuendos we carry on.

Does the mind play a role in connecting with the soul, or is it an impediment?

The landscapes of the mind have weather disturbances. Blown by senses, wavering at decision making, there are severe climate changes here. Hence, mindfulness or being aware of these fluctuations, caused by the senses, is step one to awaken consciousness. Sensitivity towards one and all is inclusive of the biosphere that sustains us and is prescribed by Buddhist meditation as a means to happiness.

As colours mingle, new shades are formed. Second and third generations soften the sharp lines of distinction. Blends replace contrasts. We need to be still and silent like a hunter waiting for the deer. We can then hear what the 'Universe' has to say. Centering ourselves brings us, to the fulcrum of the soul. When the needle shifts, the mind is blown away by uncontrollable desires and moods.

I evolve from a small-town girl to an international traveller. This is not deliberate, but circumstantial. I would have never dreamt of the 'Masters' I met, and the souls that connected to enlighten and educate me. I did not know then; I feel it now.

Awareness of myriads of selves that reside in me, is the second step to awakening. Interacting with different people, I learn about their perceptions. This developed perspective. It armed and anchored me.

The mind affects the body. Psychosomatic diseases are nothing but a 'dis-ease' of the mind. Swallowing pills, eating well and work outs at the gymnasium may work up to a point, but mind control and harmony are foundational for well-being. Can we accomplish all this without a mentor?

Our mentor is the voice of our soul, our conscience, our inner being, our true self.

Body escapes: The spirit is embodied in the body. The body, says Krishna, is the 'field'. To function well, we must be the 'knower of our field.'

At some point or the other the body dwindles to dust, and the spirit escapes. We cease to exist in the body. This does not mean we are dead. What had kept us alive is the 'spirit'. Illusion and Truth separate. We are not in the body to enunciate this.

I write as an immigrant. I also write as a native of my country of origin 'India', and my country of immigration 'Canada'. I write as a global citizen and more. Bringing experiences to paper, explains to me how we are evolving in time and space, what is changing and what is not changing. One does not have to leave culture 'A' to familiarize itself with culture 'B'. Embracing humanity is about inclusion and enhancement that comes from shared beliefs, shared knowledge and shared wisdom.

This to my mind is *'Cultural Awakening'*. Having lived in two continents and traversed two cultures i.e. east and west, I write this in unison with all my experiences and learning. It makes the writing catastrophic. Minus the specifics, 'Truths' surface. These are universally applicable in societies across the world, as they are related to human behaviour.

More than anything else, I write as a human being whose religion is 'humanity'. This is the universal religion we have forgotten. Amidst feudal wars, cultural shifts, religious differences, humanity stands tall and uninhibited. I align myself to this field. Though my journey began half a century ago when I entered the world, awakening took time. I feel I have just been born. New reality emerged as illusion lifted from relationships, so did fears and anxieties. Unabashed, I confront myself and others armed with this knowledge. This is the third step to awakening.

Nature of the Soul

"What will it profit a man if he gains the whole world, yet forfeits his soul?"

MATTHEW 46:26

The nature of the soul has always intrigued me. Believing in intuition and wondering if this has something to do with the soul, I hear a little voice firm and clear from within me, guide me. Do I act on it? Not always. Sometimes I ignore it, to my peril.

Is this the voice of my conscience or my soul, speaking in discerning tones to me? Is this the dynamism that defines me, nurtures me, makes me alive?

I do some soul searching on the platforms of human experience. The journey continues from the birth to the end. In each phase of life, I experience the soul. Yet, I cannot define it. It is my only friend, who I have and not taken cognizance of. Perhaps I was captivated by various needs of existence for example: physical, mental, emotional, familial and social needs. So, I ignored the needs of my soul. In the brief time left, I make an introspective chart and see the proportion of time each of these segments engaged me. I am in for revelations. Other than needs, it was the frivolous expectations of others, appearances and gratifications that kept me busy and away from myself. I could have saved at least fifty percent of my time had I been aware of my truth, and others' expectations of me.

Like a child in a toy store, novelty and curiosity came over me. I made space for them at the cost of my soul. Swayed by the urgent needs of the here and now, I made quick fix decisions. My steps often hurried; keeping the finishing lines in the mind, and also the enormity of responsibilities. I never really took time to look in this direction.

'Always transformation over transaction', a little voice reminded. The painting of the moneychangers on the wall became a reminder metaphor. Yet, I hurried to close life's chapters that needed reviewing. In haste I often forgot to punctuate my sentences, and my days with reflection. This truth was brought home by Dr. Eva Shipstone, the Principal of Isabella Thoburn College. She had me over for breakfast most Sundays while I was completing my Bachelor of Education and was the Student Representative. These conversations were learning experiences.

Today I look at the turns I could have taken or avoided. One is always wise in hindsight. I carry the learning and hope for some more time for enlightenment.

I find some people negate what they cannot see, hear or smell. I look for the invisibles. The five senses are tools to reach them. Then there is the sixth sense. I sense it. The voice of intuition. Some call it the 'gut feeling'.

Soul is the God particle in us.

Time and again, I become aware of its presence. In this skeletal structure there is another. It is not flesh, not blood, but 'the Spirit'. An inner light that brightens, the essence of my being, the scent in the rose, the flight of the birds.

It is both the observer and the observed.

Experiences reveal that. Hours tick away, the soul is not blemished.

What is it that it is not affected by the tide of time, circumstance and is more than meets the eye? I invite the reader to the hidden mystery of the soul, made visible to those who venture to contemplate, have faith, have clairvoyance and look consistently for answers.

Soul is the legacy we are entrusted with.

Greeks elevated 'Psyche' or the soul to be a goddess, the wife of Eros, the God of love. Hindus call it 'Atman'. Some call it "The Force," others the "Voice of Silence", still others, the "Light Within", "The Universe" and so on. Give it any name, any form, its nature remains the same in one and all. It is the kernel of all religions.

Yet, religions fight over the propriety rights of the soul.

Amidst the noise and haste, we fail to hear its voice and are veered in different directions. Awakening escapes us. Dishevelled by lack of discernment we falter, fuse reality with illusion, and wonder what the future will hold, which way to go. The fork in the road stares at us. This is a grid lock situation.

Soulful relationships may get eclipsed, but don't wither.

They are rooted in eternity, are timeless and not based on mood swings.

A Journey with His Holiness: the Dalai Lama

Picture of the Dalai Lama and me by an unknown traveler

It is Saturday 15th of October 2016, supper time. I am excited about the concert I am invited to attend at 'The Air Canada Center' in Toronto hosted by 'From Me to We' organization. I turn on the T.V. to listen to the news. It is the same old violence and war, mudslinging candidates, at the American election. Bored, I flip channels and there appears on AMP, "Kielburger, the author and founder of the book and organization 'From Me to We' in conversation with H.H. the Dalai Lama. What a coincidence! Memory triggers.

Call it chance, providence or destiny, sometimes the unexpected happens. When the Dalai Lama came to Toronto, I had to queue up for expensive tickets at the 'Air Canada Center', to hear him speak from afar. I so desired to connect with him at a personal level. It was a far-fetched dream that actualized in 2012.

Something incredible happened. I boarded the plane for Mumbai from Delhi to attend a Tata Memorial Lecture. Here my childhood friend, now a Professor at Cambridge in U.K., was speaking, and I was reading from my just released book of poetry 'Cultural Conundrums'. Keen to get there on time, I kept my fingers crossed. But the flight was overbooked. I prayed hard to be on that flight. The hostess had me wait on one side, close to the business class. Soon, she would assign me a seat. Prayers were answered.

I saw a Buddhist monk looking out of the window, from the window seat in the business class. A thought crossed my mind, "How can Buddhist monks afford business class?" He must have read my thought. He turned around.

It was the Dalai Lama looking directly at me and smiling in response. The hostess signaled me to the seat next to him. The duration of the flight was two hours. I thought, 'How wonderful, my dream has come true'. 'Two hours with the H.H. the Dalai Lama all to myself! Who would have thought of that?'

I must have been smiling to myself about my good fortune. In response to my second thought, His Holiness caught my hand resting on the armrest firmly. It was comforting. I could feel his positive vibrations settling me down. No, I wasn't nervous. Not in the least. I was ecstatic! And the interesting part is, that he never let go of my hand for most of those two hours. He held it firmly, like that of a parent who does not want the child to escape. Once or twice, I tried to slip my hand out of his grip but failed. He caught it more firmly. The energy exchange was electric. It felt as if someone was taking all my worries and dissolving them. The vibrations were so powerful, that I became oblivious of the hostesses serving drinks and food. I was on a high, in a trance. I felt truly blessed. If you were to ask me 'What did I talk about and what did he say?' I would have to scratch my brains. It was an easy conversation. A meeting of two souls! I spoke about my life in India, in Canada, about my daughter and how she was braving her challenges, but I did not have to speak at length. He was following my thought stream as none other. If peace has a definition, I felt it. Words were unnecessary. He was answering my unasked questions. I remember him saying: 'Bring her to me'. I must do that. It is so hard to get through to him now. Perhaps there will be another stroke of luck.

At some point during our conversation on consciousness and the soul, he began playing with my nose ring like a child in a playpen, distracting me from my worrisome thoughts, that were causing anxiety. A reversal of roles. He had me observe them dispassionately. I found a turn from the physical into the metaphysical plane. There was meaning and message here.

What stayed with me were words from our conversation: "Aggression and Anxiety are born out of Insecurity. You have both and are insecure," His Holiness said. He made me aware of these traits and mindfulness in controlling and ridding myself of these. "Non-Violence and Peace begin with awareness," he said. Like a true friend he had shown me a mirror in which I saw myself more clearly.

'Clairvoyance', 'Humour' and 'Love' are the attributes His Holiness displays. He is a keen listener. This makes him a good conversationalist.

I must have told him my entire life story with its ups and downs and what I did not say, I need not have said, as he understood. I felt a weight taken off my shoulders. His lighthearted humour took me to a different plane of consciousness, without my realizing it. I wondered, in a world torn by egoism how refreshing it is to meet a soul so dipped in spirituality, that is innocent and wise at the same time. Everything was a part of the fleeting landscape, in this case the skyscape from the window of the plane. My spirit was flying high with His Holiness.

'His smile melts the gloom of worldly issues. One reached a height of awareness one has never known before'. It was happening to me. At the pinnacle of a mountain looking around, but never looking down at anyone, not even my challenges, I felt happy after a long time!

He had brought the beauties of this life in the forefront metaphorically and literally. If this is what 'bliss' meant, I was experiencing it. Love streamed from his countenance and a patient smile accompanied it. His hand held mine in a firm clasp. It was reassuring, a 'Spiritual Connection' truly God sent, just when I needed it most.

I remember him saying again: 'aggression comes from insecurity, meditation and mindfulness mitigate it'. I also remember his secretary handing me his photograph for keepsake. I thought I must have him autograph it for me.

He asked: "What should I write?"

I replied, "With love from the Dalai Lama."

In his usual good natured and humourous way, he called me 'naughty' then. Nonetheless, he laughed and wrote: "To Mala Thapar with Love from 'Bigshu' Dalai Lama 23rd November 2012 on a plane to Mumbai". The photograph stands on my desk, inspiring me each day.

In our not so brief conversation, Dalai Lama had spoken of spiritual solutions. His humility was touching. His simplicity and gentleness crept in one's psyche making waves, making a difference! He was egoless. He saw the lighter side of things and yet never slighted anything. His understanding surpasses understanding itself. Spirit over matter! Peace over war! Non-Violence!

He looked into issues and beyond them. I learnt this way to observe life in those brief two hours with His Holiness.

Towards the end of the journey, he recommended I read two books: *'Shantideva'* 8th century, for 'Peace of Mind' and *'Bodhisattva's Way'* published in 1967. He wrote their names at the back of the photograph.

Under the name of the second book, he wrote 'your favorite book'. I wondered why? 'Had I at some point, read the second book?' *'Was it in another life that I had read it?'* I didn't remember it.

Once again reading my thoughts, he said, "*You'll know when you read it.*"

By now the Captain advised that we wear our seat belts. The plane was about to land. Two hours had passed so quickly. I had not felt time. The comfort of his clasp has stayed with me. His iridescent smile showered blessings and I was enriched.

While leaving my seat and drawing my hand gently from his, I made my way out of the aircraft. I turned around to have one last look at him. It was not a dream. The person on the seat adjacent to mine had clicked a few snaps of us. He said he would mail them to me. That is how I have the pictures of a chance meeting with H.H. the Dalai Lama standing on my mantel piece. I am very grateful for them. What a coincidence!

I made it to Tata Memorial Institute just in time but did not wash my hands for some time. I wanted His Holiness's energy to stay with me as long as possible. The world needs more of Dalai Lama to humanize and mitigate the conflicts egoism brings.

Meeting Mother Teresa

The rickshaw halts before 'Nirmala Niketan- Sisters of Charity.' I get down and walk towards the parlour door. It is a winter morning in Kanpur, India. The sun is balmy. It is my birthday. As is the custom in our household, each year, we try and reach out to an underprivileged segment of society.

    The door opens, as if someone was anticipating me. A frail sister walks out. I do not recognize her at first. It is only when she comes closer, do I see. She is Mother Teresa. A very small build, of gentle demeanor, she could go unnoticed but for the smile and the look of kindness on her face.

There is a lesson here: If one wants to be noticed, one must develop inner beauty that comes from good deeds.

Delighted, I greet her. She walks with me to the chapel and prays with me. There's a spring in her step. She walks fast like Yogis do. The birthday becomes special with her blessings and prayers. She takes me around Nirmala Niketan and shows me the dormitories where the sick and recovering children are in their cribs. Some sisters are feeding them, others changing their soiled clothes. They have a vegetable patch on the grounds and Mother Teresa tells me how the girls and boys grow almost all the vegetables they consume. It is an excellent learning experience in self-sufficiency. Very Gandhian in its concept.

We walk back into the parlour and Mother Teresa sits across from me and speaks to me of her life in Calcutta, the beginnings of her work and how she spread her centres in India. It is amazing how her determination and motivation, led to so much progress and success. Help came along because she had dared to walk her convictions, even though she had no clue how she would do it. It was sheer faith in the Higher Being and in herself that pulled her. A Calling of immense dimension. The sisters of charity work tirelessly, under her guidance.

Mother Teresa's leadership involves role modelling, simplicity, humility and love. These characteristics are writ large in her personality and one is moved by them.

I have seen several dirty and ill people being nursed by her, children with oozing wounds from the roadside picked up by the sisters. This question is foremost in my mind.

"I have a question", I say. Mother Teresa looks intently at me.

"How do you manage to lift the lepers with your bare hands and wash their wounds, aren't you afraid of infection from dirt and disease?" I ask.

I cannot describe the look on Mother Teresa's face. It had an apostle-like quality. What she says, confirms it. "I see Jesus in them, not the leper, not the disease or the dirt, but Jesus." When we fine tune our perceptions to look thus, all divisions resolve. Her words stay with me, each time I encounter sickness and poverty.

I have developed an appreciation and understanding of her work. This goes a long way in assisting where I can. I am no longer turned off by oozing pus from the wounds of a beggar or a sick person. It is another state in a human being!

"God has our work cut out, we need to only open our eyes and look beyond ourselves," her powerful words make way into several sisters' hearts. "There are needs everywhere, but we choose to ignore them out of ignorance or otherwise. The human in them cries out for the human in us. Do we respond?" She asks.

"It takes courage and conviction," I say.

"Yes, but the right conviction and faith first", she says. "Love others as Jesus loves you." Then again: "He loves you, love others as He loves you."

I had forgotten to love others all the time. She reminds me. It is her common denominator. At this point, I hand her the gifts I had for the children at the Centre, and she gratefully accepts them.

I ask her to write me a few words. I am carrying a book on 'Meditations' by Kahlil Gibran. First, she speaks to me, asking me a few questions about my life and beliefs. I tell her about being a Hindu, being educated by I.B.V.M. sisters in the Convent I attended. She then opens the first page of 'Meditations', and writes: 'God loves you, love others as He loves you, with love and blessings, Mother Teresa.' I notice that she has used the word 'God' in her writing on my page and has not been religion specific. She speaks about the universal religion: 'universality of love'. I also notice the soft tone, the kind words, the authenticity of them, and most of all, her willingness to accord time to speak to me. Almost an hour has passed. A blissful hour!

This is one trait all great people share. They listen from the heart and speak from the heart. She could have brushed me aside, but she listened, showed me around, spoke from personal experience, enlarged my reservoir of understanding of the sick and poor, and in doing so touched me. She holds my hand when I speak. It is a form of closeness that says: "I understand you; you count!" I shall always remember, the winter afternoon of February the 8th, 1979.

The sun felt balmy and the roses bloomed in Nirmala Niketan under the care of the residents; the look on the faces of the children, and Mother Teresa waving me from the parlour door! Her kind demeanor and gentle touch guide me in moments of doubt.

Her words resonate with the suffering humanity: *"Love others, as He loves you."*

Meeting Van Gogh

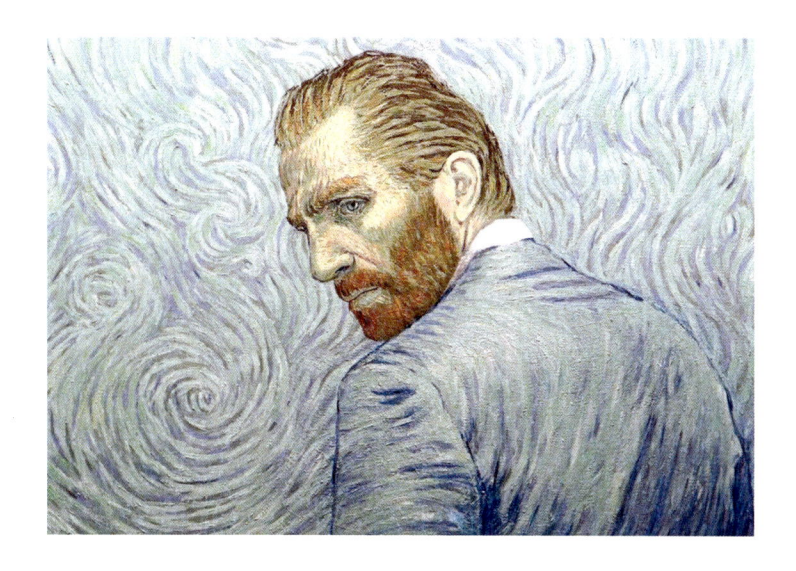

It is December the 9th, 2016. My flight from India has halted at Schiphol airport in Netherlands. Diya and I take a walk viewing the beautifully decorated stores at the airport. One catches our attention. It has a display of artwork, especially the Renaissance artists and thinkers; their art and books. We venture into the store and get busy.

One book especially catches my attention. This is of the artist born and raised in Netherlands. It is titled 'Van Gogh'. I open it to find that it contains his life, his works, the artist, close ups, his life and suffering. He challenged his mental illness. Though he never sold a painting in his life, he made some masterpieces. I am beginning to get interested. He found solace in nature not medicine. I keep coming back to the vibrant energy, light and shade, and the colour of his artwork. Come to think of it he channelled his 'Manic Depression' into a creative form and gave it a voice, a vision, a feel. He made the care of souls his mission, not earning money. He worked even when confined to an asylum. He said:

"I have nature and art and poetry, and if that is not enough, what is enough?"

At age twenty-six, he transferred his religious zeal to art. He wanted to leave a souvenir to mankind in the form of art. This he did.

I look at my daughter. She is an artist too. He was thirty-seven when he died leaving behind him a collection of art. She is challenged too. Perhaps she could take a cue from his work. I must read more about him. I want to buy the book. My euros are limited. I turn back. The price of the book is steep according to me. I return to the store deciding 'to buy or not to buy'. Then I decide upon putting it on my credit card, the only one I have and use it for necessities.

Van Gogh becomes a necessity for some reason.

His zeal, his belief in himself, love of nature and persistence, despite his failure at that time as a painter, his challenge to overcome his fears and phobias, his excesses just like my daughter's, make me decide to go for it. I reach for the book, pick it up reverently and stand in the queue. The man behind the counter has a kind countenance. "Any discounts?" I ask. "No", he says, "but I can throw in a bookmark as it is the *'WEEK OF VAN GOGH'* being celebrated."

"Good!" I think. He throws in a bookmark with Van Gogh's picture on it.

Happily, I move back towards the gate from where the flight is to take off. It has been three hours and a bit since I had water and feel parched. The inviting cafes lure Diya for a coffee and me for a drink. Water is the same price as a beer. I stop by and we calculate the Euros in my pocket and the cost of the beer and expresso. We have enough. We settle down to replenishing ourselves. I get engrossed in the book and the gorgeous pictures of his paintings. Then I turn to his portrait of himself. Expressive eyes speak of what lies behind the stark look. A troubled soul, struggling to express himself in colour and form!

Suddenly, I hear someone trying to get my attention. It is the man behind the counter who had served us the drinks. I look up.

"Is this yours?" he asks. He is holding up my RBC Visa Card.

"Yes", I reply, "But where did you find it?' I had paid him in euros.

He points to the man standing beside the counter in the queue. "He gave it to me".

I look at the man. Then I look at the open book and the picture of Van Gogh, then at the man again. Such similarity!

Is this a manifestation or my imagination? In confusion I stumble upon words: "Where did you find it Sir?"

I turn to look at the man who handed the credit card. He is still looking at me, same somber look and serenity on his face. "Is he real?' I wonder then.

Perhaps he does not understand English. I turn to the busy server who speaks Dutch.

"Please ask him where he found it".

The server looks at me after a minute, as he is serving another guest. When he does look at me, it is a look of bewilderment. He turns to where the man was in the queue. There is no one. He shrugs his shoulders. I look around. No one! It is almost time to board the flight. I would have loved to go and ask the shopkeeper whom I bought the book from. The store is far. The book is in my hand open to the self-portrait of Vincent Van Gogh, the man I just encountered. He returned my card, without which I would have been lost.

Was this his way of saying "Thank-You?"

We board the flight back to Toronto.

Van Gogh still stares at me from the cover of his book on my shelf. A reminder of the worlds we trespass. Pensive and absorbed, I reach him each time I look up. Can audio books ever take over real books?

The excesses of Van Gogh bordered on creative madness, yet they were true to his soul, to who he was.

Freedom to Explore

"For the sake of my soul, I strive not for glory, but for freedom."

REMBRANDT

Rembrandt is known for his simplicity and genius, for his humanity and love of freedom to experiment with his art and life. He is known for very effective portrayal of light and shade in his Biblical and other paintings. Though of humble beginnings he aspired and inspired other painters with his sensitivity; for example, he had a stove put in each of the model's rooms to keep them warm. A collector of art, a proponent of human values, his life like his paintings was a mixture of light and shade. His losses like his gains were many towards the end of his life. He died alone, bankrupt and impoverished with just one piece of unfinished painting: 'Presentation of Jesus in the Temple' in his room.

Fate had brought him to a point of aloneness. Here, he was preparing to meet his soul before it departed, by shedding all possessions and attachments. This way perhaps, he could focus on the entirety of the experience of the light, without any encumbrances, in a state of material impoverishment and spiritual enlightenment.

I wonder how circumstance placed him so ideally, at the point of departure, to a rendezvous with his soul. Alone-ness became the context. Meeting the soul was the subject. Was he or others like him even aware of how we are moved on the chess board of life? The universe knows what to do. We complain as we do not see the big picture. Wrapped in ignorance, we think it is we who are moving the chess pieces. Sometimes our needs are. These needs need not necessarily be physical, mental or emotional. They can also be the need of our soul wanting to speak to us.

The Prodigal Son

It is a pleasant evening at the India International Centre in New Delhi. I walk in to view a musical. The director meets me on the steps and congratulates me on my son's wedding. 'Wedding'? I ask surprised. "Yes, we got the wedding card" he says and retreats smilingly. "I don't recall getting one myself", words slip out.

It sets me thinking… then at a dinner at a friend's place later that evening, people congratulate me again. "Some misunderstanding," I tell them. I just spoke to my son and his girlfriend who has moved in with him and they denied it. One is last to know what happens to one.

Either this was a joke played on me, or a simple question I needed answers for, but evasion came my way. Distances geographic and emotional all line up and need to be addressed. Whatever is the cause of this denial; it must be addressed. He has been a loving son and a hardworking boy. What came over him?

I confronted him. "Why keep me out'? I asked.

'I invited nobody" he replied.

So, I was nobody now, and a no body eventually!

New Realization- Paradigm shift!

Keeping the parent out was neither a Western nor an Indian thing; was it a cool or a human thing?

A cultural awakening took place. The globe had taken over. Thoughts and actions changed imperceptibly as did modes of behavior.

For a parent to accept this was difficult. Great expectations from mothers, what about mother's expectations from the son?

Both continents tell the same story. 'I better not go there', a little voice within said.

I must take cognizance of the 'here and now'.

Driving back perplexed and with a heavy heart, from his place, I recalled Leonardo Da Vinci enunciating 'One has to embrace uncertainty.'

'Balance, balance, balance, the tight rope you are walking between the two psyches, the two continents – dualities must play their independent games' my soul spoke thus.

Between his partner and her expectations of him and me and my expectations of him, there lay a continent of values, ideas, expectations. Only the cultures had reversed, so did the expectations.

I understood then, there is more to it than meets the eye. Love does not go away. It gets masked for several reasons and operates on a different paradigm. We need to have patience and faith. It returns.

My soul became my friend and kept counselling me. It said: 'Relationships are agencies to teach us, sometimes allow us comfort, inspire or bring us to the 'truth of our beings.'

As time flows between the shores of attachment and detachment, the narrow gate appears, through which each must pass before they cross over.

The Prodigal Son

I had reached it and needed to *contract my expectations*, feelings, old beliefs and attachments, to enter another phase of my life.

I now began to observe the phenomena, and distancing myself from self-destructive emotions, a smile crossed my face.

Was it an observation of this life before I crossed over? Today, as I progress on the path with *self-determination*, nothing touches me to veer me away from the awakening. If it does, I contemplate on it, till I arrive at the answers. Yet, everything touches me that I need to attend to.

I am *embracing the change that uncertainty brings.*

The prodigal son has not returned, and I look at the open door awaiting his footsteps, awaiting his voice of realization. It may not come in my time, but it will come as time goes by. Of this I am certain. The universe has its laws and we seldom surrender to them willingly.

Sacrifices are made when called upon, rarely voluntarily. Tears dry up, I am grateful for the experience and the detachment it brings.

When the expectations are washed away, the unborn in us emerges. Awakened, the spiritual being continues....

Thanksgiving

'Gratitude is the memory of the heart'
JEAN-BAPTISTE MASSIEU

Harvest colours of mustard, burnt sienna, wine red and bright yellow, bathe the ground. Trees dressed in these motley colours, ignite the warmth of Thanksgiving fires. The master artist has made his canvas come alive with iridescent colours. Every tree invites a view, every pond holds a reflection. Caught amidst the turkey dinners and pumpkin pies, families and friends gather around the festive season thanking God for all that blesses their lives.

Seldom do we stop to ponder over the true meaning of 'Thanksgiving'. For me Thanksgiving is split into two halves: *'giving up'* and *'giving to'*. Both are inter-related. In order to truly give, one must give up. For giving is not artificial gifting of the surplus. It must come from within, like including a friend long forgotten, excluded or a neighbour lonely and alone, or even a stranger with no family or friends. *If a sacrifice is involved, gifting becomes more meaningful.*

Giving up negativity, anxiety, and doubt, in order to give trust, love, compassion, and care amount to gifting from one's soul. Pure intent of sharing blessings and forgoing past hurts, misperceptions, is 'true Thanksgiving' for me, as it 'provides both the giver and the receiver', like the quality of 'mercy', in Shakespeare's 'Merchant of Venice'.

The soul is enriched when both the giver and the receiver begin to 'share the vibration of love' and transcend grudges and misunderstandings that stand in the way, trading material and petty elements for the eternal and everlasting gift of humanity. Each of us can give, regardless of distance, time, funds or anything. The desire to give itself brings forth transmissions of goodwill and joy. It is the thought that matters, the intent that resonates itself with the receiver and the giver. If we only stop to think of gifting this way on this 'Thanksgiving' day, the season will deepen its colours and the energy would change for the better.

Thoughts that limit one's capacity to give, are impediments to discernment and evolution; those negative and limiting thoughts must be transcended to achieve ascendance in evolutionary consciousness. Thanksgiving is an opportunity to practice the art of appreciation and soulful gifting.

"You give but little when you give of your possessions. It is when you give of yourself that you truly give."
    Kahlil Gibran, 'The Prophet'

REFLECTION

1. Is my gift from the heart with no strings attached?

2. Is it a gift of something I no longer want, an extra I am trying to get rid of?

3. Is it a gift of time?

4. Is it a gift of prayer?

5. Is it a gift of ourselves?

Perceptions

The 'eye' that sees is not the 'I' that sees.

Many a time we rush to decisions and choices that are assumptive in nature. Upon reflection, this is because the 'eye' that sees is not the 'I'.

Trapped in contexts not of our making, conditioned by multiple factors, we tread many paths oblivious of who we are, or where we are headed. The so called 'goal setting' is often based on limited perception in a predictable environment.

What happens when circumstances change? When the unfamiliar discomforts, scales drop, hours flee, and plans don't materialize? We often enter a blame game, self- blame or debating who did what?

In our analytical thinking practice, we often lose sight of the 'I' that was not considered, as it became masked and overshadowed by the eye.

It is a matter of 'in-depth thinking' and 'superficial thinking', based on the immediate and the important. It is not just the pros and cons that need to be considered, but a deep knowledge of oneself complete with one's options, limitations, thinking tools, beliefs, strengths and weaknesses. This is then matched with the context that calls for action, the team we are working with and the trajectory of our thoughts and landscape of operation. A sincere evaluation not judgement must precede action, if success is to be encountered.

The question is: *"How do perceptions define us?"*

Perceptions based on experience make truth subjective to our individual experience. Hence, they are limited by our experience. Perceptions determined by conditioning rise out of other people's influences on us. Hence, these are stilted.

Perception of one person may not be the understanding of another. Hence, problems arise. Individual differences exist. It is not who is right and who is wrong. It is how we can understand differences and awaken to the reality of universality underlying them.

One must live with oneself 24/7 and others only a part of the time, an important part of self-evolution is development through contemplation of the 'self.'

What kind of evolutionary path are we treading? "Quo Vadis" or 'Whither goes thou?'

Words of wisdom come to mind: "To thy own self be true and you shall be false to none." – Shakespeare in Hamlet. Unless we arrive at this central point, we will not be the 'I' that sees but be the 'eye' that sees.

When falsehoods mask the kernel of consciousness, awareness takes a back seat and accidents occur. Our lives get into a maze. We begin to seek ourselves, amidst the quagmire of several contexts, we seldom pull out those pieces that define our expectations, our authenticity.

The artist paints a picture with his mind. This is not identical with the photographer, who photographs a picture, or a layman who views it. It is the viewing that makes a difference.

Perception affects the product, the conduct and the behaviour, in every walk of life.

Extraordinary Perceptions

*Beyond our horizon there are
unexplored galaxies.*

Vibrations from these galaxies sometimes enter our psyche. Moments of clairvoyance part the thin curtain that divides the visible from the invisible and the mysterious. I see different worlds. Past and present connect. History becomes a point in time where people function. It is being made every moment. I hear chiming bells, mesmerizing music. It vibrates a memory. This leads me to another cue. This time it is the sun rising from the deep blue ocean, colouring the sky with its first rays. I see forms in clouds, figures in trees, large houses with creepers of tea roses covering red brick walls.

They allude to a new way of apprehending the world viz. looking beyond the obvious, the nitty gritty, looking at one's soul in the mirror of nature, or seeing oneself as a part and parcel of something dynamic, incomprehensible but palpable, and breathing it.

*This is the field of 'pure consciousness': a
storehouse of memories.*

Extraordinary perceptions are not imaginations or dreams. They happen to us when we are awake or asleep. In these moments of consciousness, we cross human limitations, awakening the unconscious, subconscious and superconscious.

The human in us seeks. The bee is looking for honey. We for meaning, understanding and apprehending. *Enclosed in shells on a fresh line of our making, we need wings of imagination to reach out to one another and beyond.*

So, it is with consciousness and mortality. When the subconscious and the unconscious states enter consciousness, we enter the field of 'extraordinary perception'.

Heard a sound that reverberated a memory? Had a thought that brought consciousness of something happening in another part of the world? Our consciousness travels quietly but quickly, when we are still and contemplating. Sometimes I feel we are transmitters, channels, a conveyer belt that is harnessed for communicating thought and action and relating to others.

Connected to invisible realms, the quiet mind contemplates clairvoyant perception and empathic perception.

In understanding another I understand myself.

In quietude there is no categorization or compartmentalization. No divisiveness. Hence, it creates a path, a bridge that leads to a destination.

'What is that destination? Is it the same for everyone or different?'

Questions such as these are only answered in time. The restless mind keeps questioning. The curious search. The patient amongst us wait. When the moment is right, the buds flower. It's the 'inexplicable' that has always fascinated me.

'What we call 'mystery' is a 'missed story'.

This may be from our life, or lives we are connected to, or would connect to in some way for some time, or always.

While we deal with conformity and a variety of perceptions, pairing the two in a collaborative or a combative mode, we lose sight of *'extraordinary perception'*.

It is akin to 'Grace.' It is here that magic happens. This is the theatre of lives lived, and yet to be lived. It brings form to function.

Let us unclutter our minds and be open to it.

Renaissance Period and Perceptions

Leonardo's Mona Lisa Painting

*"All our knowledge has its origins
in our perceptions"*
LEONARDO DA VINCI

Leonardo connects the spiritual to the sensuous in his paintings. By highlighting the ambiguity between the spirit and the flesh, Leonardo gave his own charged meaning to: "Word became flesh and dwelt among us."[1]

Leonardo's 'To Do' lists says his biographer, Walter Isaacson were endless. I see them as a constant reminder to him, to not only to do what was needed by his art, body, physical existence but also by his soul. If we make these to do lists for our souls early in life, surely, we would be on the path of evolution. What is enigmatic to us liberates us!

---
1. John 1:14 Commentaries

REFLECTION

Make a to do list for your soul, mind and body:

Soul: ....

Mind: ....

Body: ....

Associations

"There is only one thing for which God has sent me into the world – to perfect my own character in virtue."

EPICTETUS

The Greek stoic philosopher's words come to light on our evolutionary path. It is ridden with associations. We can't escape them. But we can choose them. It is a point to be highlighted. Not allowing every vibration to house in us. Being selective to who and what we give attention.

If we invite anybody and everybody and this includes thoughts and emotions, our minds will be overcrowded with the unnecessary and the useless. To bring relevance to the picture we need to be selective. This creates space for the necessary. It is a step forward on the evolutionary path.

As one grows older, it becomes of paramount importance who and what one associates with. This affects one internally and externally. It is not about image keeping, but about *'saving the soul'*, growing the mind, acquiring knowledge and wisdom, and developing character. Interaction is key to development. Who and what one connects to calls for *discernment?*

Different bio rhythms, vibrations, energies, beings and non-beings, affect our well being as much as the food we eat, the air we breathe and the water we drink. Why is this so?

Is this because the visible and invisible worlds connect? One may be seen but the other is felt. Both have an impact upon us. We cannot see our nerves. Yet, they exist. Would we damage our nerves unnecessarily if we saw them being affected by another's aggressive and repetitive negativity? We would run from such energies that dampen and damage.

Patterns of behaviour are set early in life. They may be the result of conditioning or genetic. They may be learnt from observation and interaction or a reaction to what one has been through. Innate tendencies surface. Something within us guides us. We seldom listen to it when the false ego has us in its sway.

Possessed by possessions, we think we are omnipotent and can make or break the outside wolf.

Little do we realize that we are but the spokes of a wheel. These must be in alignment to move.

Our bodies, minds, emotions and soul must interact in harmony for our well being.

Forgetting this, we wonder why the headaches, why the illnesses? Stress settles in and brings in 'dis-ease.' It is often caused by lifestyles, who and what we surround ourselves with and give attention and space to, in our minds. We seldom look around to feel the vibrations around us. Awareness of what behaviours we are absorbing is *step one* to regulating ourselves on the path. Often awareness comes, once our associations have impacted us. Then it is hard to eradicate their effects. Cleansing of the body, mind and emotions is required to bring the mind to a still place.

A point of 'Contemplation'!

My favourite example of self-preservation and progress is one of the gardener. He pulls out the weeds and prepares the soil before planting. Then he nurtures and adds manure to let the plant grow strong. So, should it be with us. This is *step two* of awakening and staying on the path.

Unfortunately, we clutter our minds with the debris of yesteryears. This results in confusion and is especially apparent when we educate a child. She comes with a clean slate. We write in multiple expressions, emotions, thoughts, behaviours and strangle her creativity. The child thus loses interest and behaviour issues arise, grades fall, and parents and teachers wonder: 'What is wrong?'

Interrelatedness, associating learning to what is pertinent, weeding before planting make the child's life and learning a little easier. The child is not age defined. There is a child within each of us that needs nurturing.

The domain of association is not only with thoughts and ideas, but also with people. Peer pressure, gangs, cults, organizations, clubs, all these and more are hinges on which temptation leans. People get swayed. Compulsive behaviours and addictions arise. The soul is lost in the quagmire. When the individual wakes up, she finds herself surrounded by a quarry of disbelief. Her thoughts and her expectations have taken an unrecognizable turn. This is because of associations good or bad. They influence, impact and determine decisions, character and well-being.

The discrepancy between illusion and reality of our beings, then haunts us. We play catch up and end up going in circles without contemplation and right association of ideas, thoughts, actions, and people.

Associations make or break us. They send vibrations that work positively or negatively on us.

The halo effect of the prophets had a healing effect on the people. It spoke of their spiritual power. The effect of personalities and their personas is visible in the turn events take and how people form and deform. Our receptors are bombarded by millions of transmissions each day. No wonder, memory suffers. Silence and stillness put us back in form. At random we pick vibrations that please us or feed our compulsions. It is here that discernment and educated choice must be exercised. Our soul moves from the dream state of consciousness, to the subconscious, and then to unconscious and superconscious.

Shifting gears, it sees different things at different times. It is not necessarily schizophrenia to hear voices that others cannot. This could also be a paranormal experience.

Time is a tool and Soul is the guide.

We are on a path. Some of us recognize the path, others are unaware and drift. In this drift there is a pattern. The pattern repeats itself throughout our lives. Time and again we find ourselves in situations not of our making or are pulled in similar circumstances posing similar problems. Wondering if it is destiny, we either battle or give up. In either case the test goes on.

Like Christ on the cross we often cry out: "Lord, why have you forsaken me?" Hindus call it 'destiny'. Jews wait for the 'Messiah'. Shamans dance in ecstasy to reach the astral. Theosophists talk about reaching the 'Voice of

Silence' by being still and virtuous. The unconscious and the subconscious amalgamate to create a reality to the conscious mind.

It is here that I post myself and feel the vibrating pulse of different realms of consciousness. Spiritual Awakenings are the 'aha' moments of life.

Here, gleeful and happy beginnings of evolution take place. This happens when we become aware of all that happens, and all that we can make happen.

Babies smile a lot. They have a few awakening moments too. If we can only connect with them at the soul level and look deep into their eyes, we'll see reflections of innocence that is pristine. This is the sacred place, here eyes truly become the windows of the soul.

Aloneness

'It's only when we are alone, can we truly communicate''

J. KRISHNAMURTHY

To be alone is not to be lonely necessarily. Often these two words are mistakenly thought to be one and the same thing. Yet, they are very different. You are never alone. But you may be sometimes lonely. To be alone meant to be able to move and reach out in the capacity of our self.

Some of us are afraid of being alone. Thoughts and shadows scare us. Anxiety sticks its head in, and we are faced with our demons. Truth is hard to take. It stymies the lies we live at times, to keep the image going. What would we ever do without friends and clutter, constant music and video, chatter and obsessions with the material?

I pondered over J. Krishnamurthy's statement and wondered what kind of aloneness he was talking about? Years later truth dawned.

My sister and I were a continent away, streams of consciousness here and there connected us, but communication was difficult and far in between. My attempts to reach her were often met with silence. Surrounded by multiple engagements, people, to do lists, we were never alone to be able to communicate effectively. My sister confessed this before she finally passed away clutching my index finger with all the strength she could muster. It was only recently, when I went to see her in the last stages of cancer that I discovered how crowded she was by negative energies that blocked communication. I discovered then, how important it was to clear the clutter around us, mentally, socially, culturally, and physically.

We live in the shadows. These overshadow us. We need clairvoyance. It's a cultural awakening of the self and the other. To be alone meant to be free from shadows that blur.

> *"While you are alone, you are entirely your own master"* Leonardo Da Vinci

Aloneness allows one to observe dispassionately, before being absorbed by all that surrounds one. I am writing about energies and vibrations that we are surrounded by. We are losing ourselves in their frills and fancy.

Like a lone wolf crying out to the moon, let us celebrate this aloneness as a necessity, to discover and reach out to the tenets of consciousness. These will then connect with the colours of the prism of light. This is one step to discernment.

REFLECTION

Why do we crowd our minds with other peoples' misgivings?

Why are we afraid to be alone?

Are we ever alone?

Is being with ourselves being alone?

Meaningful Coincidences

You come to me in many forms.
Do I recognise you?

The plane halts at Chicago. The seat beside me is empty.

Hurried steps, taking off his coat, a man slips into the seat next to me. I get absorbed in reading my recently published book "Children of India". A few minutes pass. The flight takes off. The man settles down. He peers into what I am reading. I put the book down. "May I see it?"

I hand it to him. He flips through it, tells me about his visit to the country a long time ago, his fondness for it and a charity he funded. I am all ears.

"May I buy this book?"

"I don't know if it's on the stands."

I feel flattered by his enthusiasm.

"No, I mean from you?"

"You may have it."

"No, I like to buy books, so the author gets something"

"Many people take books free and it is my belief when you do not pay for something you don't value it. Also, the author is left bereft."

I am pleased by his generosity of thought, having no idea what is forthcoming.

"How much is it? "

"Very little when transferred to U.S. currency'" I say
He pulls out a few hundred notes, they were four of them.

"Will these do?"

"That's too much", I say.

"Please keep them, a token of appreciation".

"Are you sure?"

"Yes" he said. I work with these children in India donating computers to NGO's. I feel them in your poems." He said.

He really liked the poem: "Where did Nina go?" It is based on my daughter who is a nature lover and a wanderer, often keeping me wondering where she has gone.

Toronto is 45 minutes away. Time passes quickly as we converse about philosophy and poetry. I feel guilty about accepting his payment for the book. I have no idea what is in store for me further.

Hailing a cab from the Airport, I reach the Y.W.C.A. at Summerhill and Yonge. Next day is a workday. Eagerly I get onto the subway and from there to Adelaide St. a quick walk and I am at the office. To my surprise the company has moved in three months that I was in India. I wish I had brought some money I think, I will have to survive till I got another job. I will also have to pay the Y.W.C.A. Then it clicks. I have the four hundred dollars for my book. Thank God I have that!

How could I have assumed that my job would be there for me, after all it was a part time job held for six months? I did not know about severance pay, what other agencies I could tap into, nothing. Fresh off the boat I knew one thing, "You lose it, you look for another one, and survive somehow in the interim period."

On my way back to the Y.W.C.A., I stop by the mayor's office.

Barbara Hall is running for elections. She needs volunteers. I step in to help, fighting my anxiety. She throws a party for the volunteers after a few days. It is here that I meet my next employer.

I am thankful for the four hundred U.S. dollars to tide me through the lean period.

This brought awakening of waking up from the assumptive world to the world of faith. It was a turning point, a bend in the road. Surely, someone was preparing me for what lay ahead. So, it is at the end of life. There is no need to be keyed up about the unknown. Exploring the unknown can sometimes be better than the humdrum of the known realm. After all we are here to evolve. If so, fear is that one layer of the onion we must shred. Yes, we cry sometimes as we peel layer after layer.

Fear and Love

Diya blissfully swims in the soul of Lake Huron

While fear of knowing oneself restricts knowledge of the soul, love creates an affinity towards the 'God particle' and coupled with reverence, it makes a contact with one's soul. This then can be developed with frequent meditation, mindfulness, chanting, introspection and soulful connections. As the being evolves, it feels the pace and the peace in reaching out to the light within. When love becomes a force, fear diminishes, and soulmates arrive. However, patterns may revert, and we may drive them away. Consciousness helps us to recognize and retain soulmates. The conflict is between the outer mind that is fear borne, and the inner soul that knows, and is certain in its faith.

Encounters

"Self-knowledge is the beginning of wisdom. In self-knowledge is the whole universe, it encompasses all the conflicts of mankind"
KRISHNAMURTHY

Sometimes we lose ourselves in the nitty gritty and need an encounter to wake us, to be who we really are… for our true selves to emerge. It was one such moment at the grocery store upon meeting a friend who inspired my true self, I put pen to paper again. Returning from a tumultuous trip from India where a lot was done, and a lot still left to be done, I had buried writing by procrastinating it. A little voice gnawed at me, ideas came and went, and experiences dwelled for a while then left me. I mended a few family bridges, especially where weak links were breaking bonds.

There was a lot of negativity surrounding my sister struggling with cancer.

She had lost her voice literally and metaphorically. To get her voice back meant psychological healing along with determining the cause of the loss whether it was larynx or something more.

There was one answer; to build hope, an atmosphere of good cheer and positive vibes. Fair weather friends had left. Husband, son, daughter-in-law, all seemed to be waiting for her end. She sensed this and a sense of futility set in.

This is how it happened: While there was insecurity outwardly, she turned inwards to find security. She had begun to free herself from created expectations, images and beliefs. In gradually separating the disease and her relatives from her real self, she found the space to smile dispassionately.

To experience this truth, is to touch the unseen hem of consciousness, it took strength, courage, creativity. She managed herself well.

The observer in her embraced the change and accepted it to connect with the soul.

It is a long and arduous course; life's teachings etch deep down to pave a way going forward!

Transformational Leadership

'Be the change, you wish to see in others...'

GANDHI JI

We do not seek experiences, experiences seek us. Gandhi's mentor Gokhale brought Gandhi from South Africa to India. He knew if there was one person who could win over the British Empire, it was Gandhi. Without violence, India gained her independence primarily due to Gandhi's Sarvodaya and civil disobedience movement. His social justice extended to removing the tag of caste system from the Dalits and renaming them as 'Harijans' or people of God, instead of being called 'untouchables' by the upper three sections of society viz. Brahmans, Kshatriyas and Vaishyas.

One of our workers at home was a Dalit. We did not see him as that. His tall stately countenance became a bedrock for us and won our trust. He worked quietly and stood strong. In my growing years he became a trusted friend. 'Rajput', that's what he called himself. He cleaned the house immaculately in the dusty industrial town of Kanpur. His moustaches curled giving him an air of regality. His cultural heritage showed in his behaviour. He measured up to whatever task was assigned to him, thus proving himself to be a born leader. Gandhi had seen this humane face of the Dalit. He had recognized the damage done to humanity by segregation and non inclusiveness, having faced it in South Africa when he was thrown out of a first-class compartment despite having bought the train ticket.

I still recall the look of statesmanship and stewardship in Rajput's eyes. This always made me wonder why he was working at our house, and not on some throne of importance. I had to ask him.

"Leadership is a quality, not determined by place or portfolio but by character," he told me. His words stuck to my mind. I applied them in daily life with great results. Practising on his dictum made me the Captain of the school team and later the President of my college. In both these portfolios interacting with students and staff was involved.

His advice: "Role Model, quietly work, trust so you may be trusted, know your limitations and work on your weaknesses and strengths."

This helped a lot. Then one day he left us. Where he went, why he went, I do not know. Who was he? I wonder sometimes. The house was never the same without his silent strength. I was humbled and learnt my first lesson in 'humility'. From my humble mentor I learnt: *Leadership is not related only to those in power or position.*

Humility is its garb and honesty its creed.

I learnt that as the shepherd leads his flock, the leader in us practices role modelling as his message. Leadership is an inner calling to contribute, fix and resolve both people related and other issues. Hence, we move from transactional leadership of everyday nitty gritty, handling routine to transformative leadership embracing changes that creep on us surreptitiously, embracing them and making a difference.

Education needs transformation more than mere transaction. Our schools are made to run as corporate offices without a kernel of transformation. Agreed, the world is moving that way. Yet, in the formative years humans need more than strategy. They need leaders who not only point the way but *'be the way.'*

I took a course in 'Leadership Training' in my early years of teaching. This was facilitated by Fr. S.J. Wirth. I wondered why he gave so much power to group dynamics. By the end of the course, I realized much of the magic in the training, the 'Aha' moments came from interaction between groups both assenting and dissenting feelers. Those were areas of 'growth', provided we did not take the comments personally.

We often ignore the 'person' within us who is evolving too. When we defend ourselves, we close the door to growth and clairvoyant vision, thus hampering our evolution. Introspection is necessary for transformation, and if this precedes transaction, human error takes a back seat.

Gandhi knew that. His only armour was his 'will power'. This coupled with his love for humanity and non-violence made him win wars without weapons. His pure soul was unafraid. Hence, there seemed to be no need of weapons.

His soul became a formidable weapon. Hence, it took the entire British empire to keep Gandhi in poverty and the nation on the path of self-sufficiency.

When he was shot, he *forgave* his killer Nathuram Godse. Christ did the same saying: *'Father forgive them, they know not what they do.'*

It comes down to 'consciousness of the self and the other.'

It is the soul that shone through adverse circumstance and left a mark on the followers. It rendered a message for humanity and of 'humanity.'

Forgiving is a part of the process of transformation.

Fragmentation

"What is the narrative?" she asked me.
"Fragmentation", I said. "Brokenness and issues around it."

I don't remember when I became a collector of fragments of broken selves.
I could sense life in its varied fragments crying out to me at different times, and in different places. I would stop the rickshaw on my way to school to turn off a running municipal tap, that everybody used but nobody turned off.
Education became 'application'.
Broken and unattended, these fragments of garments used and abused go unnoticed. Even today, I see people straddle them, move away, ignore and carry on. The road bends. Same scenes repeat themselves across continents. Totally unaware of others, just themselves and their agenda, sometimes not even that, being pulled in different directions, I see humanity suffer.
I am a part of the suffering, a part of the system *'that waits for another to change.'* Realization is a far cry. Endeavor in the right direction is misunderstood and aligned *'to getting and spending.'* Minimalism not consumerism. I want to make minimalism a mind set. Essentials. Less to worry about. More freedom at hand. Nothing to lose!

Space is created. Few friends, fewer associates, less entanglements, more time for the soul. The idea is to make the soul my friend. This takes *undivided attention*. How can attention run in different directions and yet, be contained and directed exclusively focussing on the soul?

There's very little known. Still less ventured.

Amidst forests I am looking for 'a tree' whose colour and shape elude me. It has no colour and no shape. I must still find it. I am looking for my soul. Why it got embodied and how can I achieve all that it aspires for?

Freedom

Manik jumps into the French river with faith and courage.
Photo credit J.M.K.S

Let me free myself from the tentacles of the slavery of habit, conditioning and judgements.

I experience freedom to be two-fold: Freedom from habit and freedom to evolve.

Both are equally essential and need clarity. Waiting does not imply idleness to my mind. It is a mindful pause.

I realized I could not have freedom to create unless I was free from entanglements. This was an important realization after four decades of living a life of habit. I wished realization had dawned earlier and saved me time and effort from always trying to meet other peoples' expectations.

Little did I know, I had to search my soul for the answers.

The longing of the soul to merge with the divine is uncovered, when I open myself to experience. In the early years, some of us are misled and take freedom to do as one likes. This is a misinterpretation of freedom and is counter productive.

The Soul is our mentor, when we nurture it in silence.

In stillness we can hear the birds fluttering their wings, understand their language and connect with the universe.

Education of the Heart

I gaze through the window, at the leaves on the trees outside. It is fall again. An amalgamation of colour greets me. The lyrics of Louis Armstrong's song "What a wonderful world" come to my mind. It is the first period in the morning. There is a readiness to receive amongst the students in the classroom at St. Joan of Arc High School, in Barrie, Ontario. The lesson plan indicates encouraging students to participate in the food drive and answer the questions pertaining to 'why' and 'how' of participation. I love that! It is something real, active and much needed by society. Moreover, it's an opportunity to build empathy.

Stephen Covey's eighth habit of effectiveness comes to mind. But this is not what I am thinking. I am taken back to my regular teaching days at Loreto Convent in Lucknow, at St. Columba's Delhi and St. Mary's Convent, Kanpur in India.

I share this story with the students on the 'why' of the Food drive. It is a firsthand experience in a country where food is produced and exported and yet, there are many people dying of starvation.

Consciousness shifts.

I am a teenager, walking down an ally to catch my bus to school. On the way, I see street urchins dig deep into waste bins to get remnants of leftovers, thrown by restaurant staff. Something in me stirs. It is the look of anguish on the innocent faces of the urchins at not finding scraps in the dustbin, then the look of cheer at finding a rotten tomato. Invariably, I end up giving my lunch bag to them. As time goes by, they wait for me to pass that way. My mother packs another lunch bag for me, then another, then another. But this can't go on, something more must be done. I speak to Sister Margaret I.B.V. M, the Principal of the school. The human factor kicks in. We begin food drives, a free kitchen, every Friday. Each student brings in a potato, a tomato or a loaf of bread. A fruit a day for the daily giving. Education of the heart begins. Gradually we adopt one family per class in the slums on the banks of the river Ganges. We maintain a health register, education, employment, etc. and spend time with them volunteering instruction.

It is surprising how much resilience they have. Each time we come out having learnt more from their experience, than what we went to impart.

The students get this. In the beautiful country of Canada, it is hard for anyone to imagine that there is no elbow space in cities like Calcutta. One must feel hunger pangs and lack of space to value these great gifts.

The class gets motivated and engaged. They begin to unfold strategies for participation in the drive and see a reason behind it. Its not just about quenching physical thirst and hunger.

I take them a step further. It is this step that keeps motivation going. It is the emotive learning step of building 'empathy', of sharing and caring, of sacrificing and transcending.

"What happens when you come to school without breakfast?" I ask.

"We are constantly thinking of food and going to the cafeteria and cannot concentrate," they answer.

"And what if you cannot buy from the cafeteria?" I ask.

"Then we ask another to buy for us", is the reply.

"And if they refuse?" I ask.

"Then we're stuck," they say.

"Well, this is exactly what is happening in the world and one of the reasons for crime".

"There is no shame in being hungry and seeking fulfilment. There is shame in not sharing and letting another go hungry," I say.

To close the first part of the lesson, I'll give you another real-life example.

It is the year 2009. I am about to enter the café at Hart House, at the University of Toronto. I frequent this place all the time. But today I am approached by a bystander, a student with golden hair and blue eyes; he wears a look of fatigue and helplessness.

"May I please ask you to buy me a muffin?" he says. "I haven't eaten since morning".

His plea is unusual. I have never heard it before at the U. of T. cafeteria. Yet, it is genuine and strikes a chord. "Sure", I say, and we go in. He gratefully accepts the muffin and gobbles it down. "Can I get you something more, maybe a meal?" I ask, while reading the menu pasted on the wall. I turn around and he's gone. Mesmerized, I wonder if I was being tested or it was a real experience.

The look of gratitude on his face and the face of those little urchins in India has stayed with me. Hunger has no denomination or nationality. It is not geographically bound. The students get that. "What a great way to start Thanksgiving", someone utters in the class. My purpose for the day is fulfilled. We connect. The 'human' in us is stirred. *Consciousness awakens!* I have connected with my soul and those of the students.

Ass- u- me

"The mind in its own place can make a hell of heaven and heaven of hell."

JOHN MILTON

Tall buildings stream the sidelines of St. Clair Avenue in Toronto. Attractive stores with still more attractive merchandize. I rush past these. No interest. Then a bookstore heralds me. Hidden in one corner with vines creeping on it, it is just the place one can hide in with a book. I walk in. I like a book on gardening. When I open it, it turns out to be linking life to gardening. It speaks of developing a garden, by weeding before planting. I comprehend this: 'What do I need to weed before I start afresh?'

'Assumptions' is the answer that comes to my mind. They cause so much distress.

In the Japanese language there is a word *'kuuki yomenai'*. It means a person who cannot read between the lines. This occurs when instead of listening, one assumes. Often all of us 'assume' from our individual or cultural point of view.

Canada is a new country to me. I must step with care. This I do, and proceed on the path of learning and working, socializing and educating my children, daily within the framework of timely run schedules. This is possible when we do not assume that the other person will understand where we are coming from.

To me the word reads thus 'ass u me'. Assumptions often do just that. For example, when landing in Toronto and getting the first job I applied for, my employer asked me if I had 'S.I.N.'? He did not use the word 'card'. Nor did he use the article 'a' or 'the'. I was totally confused and wondered about 'sinning'. It was hilarious!

Both of us had assumed what each one meant, until we questioned our assumptions.

PART TWO

*And when a man sees that the God in himself
is the same God in all that is,
he hurts not himself by hurting others:
then he goes indeed to the highest Path.*
SRI KRISHNA 28:13 BHAGAVAD GITA

'Brahm and Bhram'

'Brahm' is the *Creator* and 'Bhram' is the *Illusion*. Both forms of creation overlap. The world of illusion, 'Bhram', covers the real world of creation, 'Brahm'. If we are not clairvoyant, 'bhram' will shroud our senses and move them from real to virtual. This leads to confusion in a world moving towards virtual reality.

To recognize and differentiate between the two, is to awaken wisdom. This leads to the path we need to travel in order to progress in our evolutionary cycle.

It involves awakening three areas of Consciousness: Soul, Body and Mind.

They are not distinct from one another as they influence each other and are present as 'One Self' in oneself.

Why do souls come into the world? Why do they manifest into bodies and go through mortal motions? Is there a purpose to Creation more than proliferation? If self-realization is the goal, how can we achieve it in a temptation-ridden world? Questions such as these trouble my mind.

The seeker in me flips several books, pivots to like-minded people, restless and eager for answers; the journey takes me through different experiences with numerous agencies garbed as friends, relatives, associates and strangers. Sometimes I get lost in the maze of the expectations and relationships begin to own me. I cede. Later on, I realize that I need to extricate and resume my journey. I had halted too long at one station. This realization is once again an awakening.

I realize: Answers did not lie in enmeshed relationships, personal or professional. Profit and loss become speculative and illusory concepts, formed in the mind and actualized with intent. They take a toll on the soul.

When the shell cracks, the butterfly flies out. The 'shell' can be interpreted at different points of existence, differently. It can be a mind set, an emotional fixation, an obsession or more. It is best not to tag it, but to feel it, embrace it and accept it. In doing so no force is applied. There is a rhythm to formation and dissemination.

Awakening to this consciousness is the key to creating bio rhythms that blend and bear the ups and downs with equanimity. This has been my experience.

Body is an external shell housing the spirit and the mind. Getting out of it is as much a struggle, as it must have been getting into the illusive game of 'bhram' and meeting hard core expectations of an ever-disseminating world.

Transitions are moments of evolution and awakening.

When all seems to be lost, a new beginning is on the way. Awkward moments need to be addressed, reflected upon and aligned with inner growth.

Something in me stirs when I hear soulful music, have soulful relationships, venture into soulful living. The 'how' of it escapes me. The 'why' of it questions. The 'where' of it beguiles. I am beginning to journey inwards. Stillness is my guide and silence my tool. My soulmates are quintessential in this journey.

Caught in being and becoming, of worldly trappings, I had not heard the quiet voice of the soul at times. It was lost in the distracting noise around, seeking my attention with the same fervor. When upon contemplation, I did apprehend it, my soul took a leap forward and I learnt that by acquainting myself with the light within, I could enter the realms that lay around and beyond with knowledge and empathy.

Third Eye Perceptions

James Redfield in his book 'Celestial Prophecy' speaks about the human potential to 'expand and create a new planetary evolution'.

It is imperative, we join in to co-create.

Decades ago, I read and reread 'Dear and Glorious Physician' by Taylor Caldwell. I was touched by the story of St. Luke. He did not know then that he had the 'power to heal', other than that of a physician. He had developed clairvoyant perception. This empowered his healing faculties.

We may not be aware of it and yet, be developing the third eye that looks beyond the parochial. Fascinated by the 'halo around the heads of prophets and saints', I delved deeper. Was it related to contemporary terms like 'positive energy fields' resulting in 'healing auras'? I found myself getting engrossed in the subject.

Medical science has proved that miracles occur. Just as distant objects are seen with telescopes, X-Rays and C.T. scans, showing us what is happening inside our bodies, 'Anu drishti Sidhi' the Sanskrit term takes us to another level. Anu is for atom, 'drishti' is for insight and 'sidhi' is the power to develop X-Ray eyes that look into the hurting atoms for healing purposes.

Seeing the unseen is venturing into the unknown.

Hindus call it: 'third eye perception' and it is 'all pervasive consciousness'; the key to educating the active mind, the thinking body, and maximizing spiritual potential.

Current government investigating tools in advanced countries have begun to use remote perceptions of what is happening beyond their line of vision, to detect people on the wanted list and thus investigate crimes. They call it 'Extra Sensory Perception'. Technology and artificial intelligence are mere tools. They sometimes masquerade the spiritual aspects of healing.

When I recline my thoughts and connect the dots across time zones, I sense the palpable aspects of *'clairvoyant perception'*. This is 'Grace' bestowed by faith, experienced by St. Thomas Aquinas, Ramakrishna, St. Paul and others in different periods of history.

They reached 'a place of beatitudes' by this awakening. It needs transcendence which creates space for its descent. And transcendence starts by forgoing 'wants' not 'needs'. How one interprets them is another matter.

Since the word *'yoga'* means connecting the human to the 'divine', we need to develop faculties of perception. For this, we need to transcend the seven gates of temptation that trap us.

The light thus reached is what the Taoists call: *'The Force of bright light that connects to the primal'*.

I was fortunate to experience this light, when I healed from a relapse of typhoid fever at age sixteen, despite the doctor having given up. It made me sit up and record the brilliance of this experience. I wrote behind the Oxford pocket dictionary by my bedside:

> *'Dressed in white you come to me, your thought is so luminous, how much more would your company be?'*.

This was the beginning of my fascination with writing and my journey into the unknown realms. I was granted a second chance at life. This truth was made known to me prior to the doctor confirming it, on his 'house visit' the following day.

The Celtic in Ireland link spectacular perception to early morning and twilight zones. They call it the *'second sight'*. For them, it refers to luminosities, auras, and is sacred. I affirm this, as I experience the compelling need to write each morning and thoughts and words flow on the paper. Am I discovering my soul and treading another domain?

Desired Outcomes

The power of intent works for us when we focus on the desired outcome.

When there are issues to be resolved democratically, especially from a position of power, I find it very useful to apply the techniques my father used.

He would make us sit around, present real-life scenarios and ask, "What do you think?" "How would you resolve this?"

This stimulated our thinking process and 'what if' scenarios. It helped us to distinguish between emotional and logical decisions and their supposed outcomes. Then he would move to desired outcomes and what it would take to reach these.

These were the action steps. Thinking became objective, strategies were laid out, and actions steps provided by us children. Hence, ownership of the problems and their solutions lay with us. Once that was accomplished, motivation was on its way.

I practised this with the staff and students in professional and personal life and discovered that the most challenging ones come around. The need lay in getting people involved in the situation. The onus of the solution lay with them. So did the responsibility of the desired outcome.

I also observed that children are spontaneous. Their unbridled intellect spoke fearlessly, unless it was harnessed in fear not faith. We are naturally trusting, till circumstances prove otherwise or fear sets in. Similarly when we act upon our soul's dictates, we take the responsibility for the desired outcomes.

What could be more beautiful than a trusting and faithful heart!

Truth

Truth is the uncovering of lies
It is the kernel in the fruit
Often not apparent at first sight

Truth is not a perception. It often bases itself on a perception. Perception in turn arises from conditioning, experience, learning and prejudice. It can be false.

Only when the mist from the mountains moves and clears the sky is 'Truth' revealed. Then the light of consciousness descends. This is a transformative experience. It is a paradigm shift. We discover ourselves and our goals, the world around us wears a new look imbued with the freshness of a new sight. We distinguish 'truth' from 'perception'. It is self-evident.

The 'dew' we come upon is a gift. It is 'Grace'. We can't mess with it. When we try to question it, it dismembers. It requires faith and more… to experience 'Truth'. To live it is a life-long mission. To face it, an act of courage. It is not self-serving nor forgiving. Mankind's greatest fear and trial is 'facing the naked truth' and living it.

For the mission to be successful, commitment is needed. For commitment, we need to transcend the nitty gritty that entangles our consciousness and keeps it from rising to new heights.

Each day becomes an endeavour to view new sights with insight.

Let hindsight not block us then, but help us build foresight, lest we stumble in our commitment and in our aspiration!

Understanding Oneself

This is the hardest thing to do. We wear blinkers when looking at ourselves. We see what we want to see, not what is and what is not.

The life we lead is not the one we necessarily intended to live but were conditioned to live. No one knows at the beginning of their lives, where they will be the next year and thereafter. Yet conditioning of the mind, emotions, circumstances, and expectations crowd in imperceptibly; not only do they define us but they embark us on a journey. We make choices based on our patterns of thinking; we even turn corners right or left automatically.

Seldom do we stand back and wonder why do we make the choices we make, what lies beneath these choices and who is the architect?

I see a charpoy where my grandfather is seated. He is telling this little girl stories.

One story each night! I listen eagerly, my chin cupped in both my hands, leaning forward to catch every word. Stories from Panchatantra, Aesop's Fables, The Count of Monte Cristo, Mahabharata, Ramayana and more. Then it is over, he closes the book and asks me: 'What was the moral of the story?'

Then again: "How can we apply it in life?"

This is the best education I ever got. It connected me to great minds and linked them to my mind. It invigorated 'thinking'.

He steps in: "Karne se pahle soch le har kaam ka anjaam", he says in Pharsi; in other words, 'think of the consequence before taking a decision.'

His words come to me, when I reflect upon my mistakes. Why did I not think of the consequences? Was I even aware of them? Often, it is too late. The strings are pulled, and the curtain is down. Patterned behaviours often pass the baton to another and another. Humanity errs!

Are these the learning curves in the school of life?

My Soul

I need you now
I needed you then

When all is done
I step into a fresh terrain

not knowing how
not knowing when

you are the voice
i search for now
through the mist and rain

will I ever find you?

in this motley train
will my search be in vain?

Realization: Today I feel I am reborn to discover and uncover another spirit within me, who has patiently waited all along to surface. It is my *'soul'*.

The Significance of Pause

Pause is that sacred space which holds revelations to Truth

Everyone likes to rush… but how many like to 'hush the rush' and pause? What is pause? Is it a few minutes of silence? Is it 'think time', 'processing time' or 'reflection time'? To my mind it is all this plus more. It is an essential feature of the functioning of the brain, the spirit, a consciousness to arrive at "Truth".

Why is everyone in a state of mental anguish, in a rush to judge, from a place of false perceptions that seem right, but become crutches to lean on? Why is silence sometimes pregnant with the noise of perceptions, unmasked, waiting to be lifted like mist from the morning air?

These are but reflectors of an image maintained, a life lived, an association with people or thoughts harboured for a long time. It is only in the shaking of these misgivings, that we begin to truly observe.

To arrive at "Truth", we must pause at the threshold of our perceptions and examine them. Then become the observer and the observed, allowing space and time for truth to percolate, through the hourglass.

Everyone likes to be right. This shrouds "Truth". It is only when we pause to probe ourselves, that we uncover wrongs that need to be righted. It is like editing a document by revision. This is meaningful. This is beautiful. It allows the brain to process information. Like a dance, it is taking a step back, before taking a step forward, making way for the other to uncover too.

Somewhere in the stream of post-modern consciousness, noise has become a constant barrage. We allow it to make dents in our inner world without 'pausing'. 'Noise can be noiseless' tinkering of thoughts, haunting memories and daunting words. These have become the new normal. Yet they are not. Noise from outside us, clashes with voices from within. These need to be heard.

Speech without pause becomes a run-on sentence harbouring obsession, arriving at confusion. Yet, we allow this because we are not giving credence to the importance of 'pausing', of being, not necessarily 'becoming', of 'travelling', not necessarily "arriving"!

Sometimes there are no finishing lines. There is no period at the end of a sentence. There is an exclamation mark. An 'aha' moment. Can our life be so fluid and beautiful that it ends with an aha?

People swallow pills to curb excessive behaviours. These help to a point. Eventually, it is the understanding and the will to self-correct, restrain, to get in the gap and to pause that matters. Reflection over reaction, thought over words!

'I may never arrive, but the pleasure of travel will be mine.'

Hope

'It is not the patient's job to make the world understand, but the world's job to step back and let the patient speak in languages the world has yet to learn'.

Unfortunately, this does not happen when one is helplessly lying at the mercy of the medical faculty, caregivers and others. One often becomes an object. Once tagged with an incurable disease, the patient begins to be treated as a fossil for experimentation, and his/her human rights are written off silently.

Patience is seldom an option for the patient. The hegemony of the system, the so-called relatives and well-wishers take over. It is an assumptive game of power and control. Here, management of the disease and the patient not the cure, become paramount. Following guidelines and procedures, to get through it and beyond it, becomes paramount. Is the human left behind as a bag of bones waiting for decalcification? Does she become an object? What is her hope if we do not wear the bifocal lens of evolution and empathy?

As a world community, we need to think with our hearts and minds, not objectify people when they are down. This is what inclusiveness and democracy are about.

Does a child have a say in her upbringing? Does a patient have a say in her treatment? Does a student decide her curriculum of study? Is the pace of the world ever connected to deciphering the end recipients?

My daughter is the most courageous person I have ever known. She battled fibrous dysplasia of the skull, since age eleven. It was a little known cranial skeletal disease that caused compression of the optic nerve, loss of sight in one eye and further surgical complication of ptosis of the left eyelid, disfiguring her face.

She struggled to complete her O.A.C. cheerfully. Determined and enthusiastic, never missing a class but looking forward to interacting with her teachers and other students with gusto. She wasted no time in taking her degree at U. of T.; and then a diploma in 'Hospitality and Resort Management.' She needed to keep learning. It made her feel included in the larger fabric of humanity that pondered over issues of the mind. In an academic environment, she felt engaged intellectually. While people around questioned her prospects of landing and holding a job, I encouraged her.

My question is what became of her hard work and persistence? How did the institutions come forward in placing her? Was she - and others like her - a passing phenomena for who the university and institutions took no responsibility? Was attaining a piece of paper, called the degree, the end of the responsibility of the institution? How she runs around flaunting her resumes. No one hires her. If they hire her, they politely fire her. Do I have to start a business for her which others, not she, can manage? What happens after me? Does she become a victim to be exploited?

What I am writing about is staying connected with the soul and the enlightened mind within each of us; the God particle within us.

If education is not only about landing a job and making money, then why is it so competitive, exclusive and divisive? Does it favour those who are apt to be acceptable by society's standards of what is appropriate? Do the crumbs of society living on the fringe, literally on the edge, ever get a voice? If so, why is it shut down and people turn away as truth is hard to decipher, and still harder to comply with? It promotes guilt in some comfort zones and is unsettling for those who wish to be undisturbed by its cries.

It's an awareness issue, before complacency sets in society. I was aware that she was battling with medical challenges and needed to transcend them for a higher end. Both inwardly and outwardly she was and is struggling with the disease. This includes being accepted and acknowledged by prospective employers.

Psychological issues arise, when exceptionalities come to be objectified by society by segregation and commodification.

Education of the heart can help mitigate these to some extent. Diya is a voice in the crowd. She has the courage to be vulnerable. To present her work in the class, to the class, is the dream she lives for. I often audit her classes to see how she performs and am not disappointed. She writes her examinations independently. She walks her path herself, gets lost in the subway and then returns, then does it again. Sure, some people look at her askance. They wonder at her seeking, her ability, her passion and drive. They doubt its end results. I commend her each time, she smiles an acknowledgement. She stands up to those who scoff and enquire, doubt and delay a response. I am amazed at the strength she draws from her soul.

I have my nervous moments because she is vulnerable and impulsive. These are my concerns. I can caution her, but not infect her with my fears and anxieties. That would diminish and stunt her. It takes thought to provide her 'exceptional soul' with its legitimate freedom and not curb its flight.

It becomes a daily challenge to work with sensitivity and containment, to respect the sanctity of her being, and of others like her. These people struggle regularly in areas, most of us are not even aware of. We can make their journey less cumbersome by being open not closed to their social need to connect as equals not as exceptionals. The years she spent at the University of Toronto, St. George's campus, taught us lessons in 'Perceptions.'

We learnt that *'perceptions were fluid and not fixed'*. We learnt that when perceptions become fixed, they become fixations and prejudices. We tried to meet every perception from a rational point of view, deciphering requirements from opinions. This protected our psyche, as we worked on what was needed and not who thought what. We made headway.

There are other people who are struggling as I write this. Silence greets exceptionalities. They are zoned out of the mainstream. We need to encourage them to feats they can achieve, and not limit them by putting tags around their social insurance numbers, tags that define them as much as their affliction. In doing so, we cripple them by not gauging their inner strength, by not giving them a chance.

For example, Diya's face lit up when volunteering at Royal Ontario Museum at the diamond exhibition. A lady came up to her and said, "How knowledgeable you are, I am impressed". I overheard the comment. It validated her. Similarly, publishing her book of poems, going to the Poetry conference in Washington D.C. where she read her works and got a feedback, all these were small steps with huge emotional returns. She had to walk the rope as an able person, fortified with positive experiences, with love and care and had to have someone there for her to stay on the path. It was a step I took voluntarily and have never regretted it.

The lens we look through, is as important, as the hand we extend.
It not only defines the other, but it defines us.

Women's Stories

Amidst the applause, the tears, the smiles, the high rises and the sun setting at a distance, she dropped the mortal fabric. *"Love is all that matters"* were her last words. They came hard but clear. Her life was lived at different planes at different times under different circumstances. The sun went down, save one streak of orange.

I had watched her grow, helped her in doing her homework, and life bubbled, smiled sweetly. Then frustrations in marriage and motherhood crept in. Patterned to give in, to comply, she continued. Each time she spoke up, or voiced her mind, she was looked at disagreeably by the male fraternity. The deficits in her life stressed her. They took the form of 'cancer'. There was no family history here. But the history created by wrong decisions - hers and other peoples - and worse still, submitting to and staying with these decisions, living them as a punishment made her soul go wry.

She managed cancer. What took her life was 'Cardiac arrest'. The shock and disbelief of her very own flesh and blood, the man who she believed in and lived with 'under the pretence of care and good stewardship' would so disappoint her. Her only son, who she looked up to and trusted to be by her side would become a source of constant concern to her and eventually both factor in bringing her life to a quick end. "Look they are talking about costs - not me," she said helplessly from the hospital bed. I turned to them, then to her. There was a disconnect. This troubled me immensely. I tried to take her with me to Delhi in an ambulance. Her oncologist was here. I cared enough to do that. She was so eager to come too. But no! I was firmly denied this opportunity by her husband and son. They knew she would die, if she was removed from the hospital. Yet, they took her home. There were no medical facilities available here. They let it happen and without her consent or informing me, her only blood relative.

Her passing away diminished me in ways more than one. It diminished all women and men who are subject to being objectified by society's prowling sections, be they relatives, friends or others. She left a lot to ponder upon. No one knows what happened, as communication is at an end. No one will know.

What matters now is praying for and reaching out to as many people as possible who share the same fate quietly hoping, someone will come and rescue them.

Who will that someone be? Let's awaken ourselves to this reality and hear the stirrings of these souls. The vulnerable depend upon us. Will we measure up? Will we be that someone?

Her soul looks brightly to me. It smiles saying: 'Didi, I am going to a better place, I don't feel age, just peace, a deep peace that no one can stir.'

She realized the eternal truth of 'detachment in love'. A child walked by and laid a yellow marigold by her funeral pyre, sanctifying 'womanhood', while her family wrestled with their prejudice. She was my sister. The child was a stranger.

As I lit the funeral pyre, which was agonizing, I could hear her whisper: *"When the going gets tough, the tough get going."* Her sweet smile soon became a memory, as smoke devoured the flames.

Once again, it was the known greeting the unknown. Nature became a bond. Like the Ganges river flowing beside the cremation ground, time flowed ceaselessly. Mortality met eternity on its way.

Remnants were not her ashes, but prejudiced and self-serving people who hastened this end with their lack of sensitivity and misperceptions. For them, it was 'the end'. For me, it was a beginning, a realization! Let her imposed death be an awakening of other souls on their multiple journeys!

Mystery

"Be open to mystery, not everything needs sharp lines"
LEONARDO DA VINCI'S NOTES
TO HIMSELF IN HIS "TO DO" LISTS

We tend to box everything and label it. Can we label the soul or box it? There is no such thing as 'my soul is different from your soul.'

Soul connection is the only pure connection. Thelma, the protagonist in Marie Corelli's book, 'Thelma' says: *'Love me for my beauty sake, love me not then, love me for my youth sake, love me not then, love me for my soul sake, love me then.'*

It is permanence and this deeper quality of love that always attracted me. It is not infatuation, not need based or greed based, but *soul based*. I read this book a few times. The answer lay in making one's soul a friend and seeking soul mates.

The Landscape of Ageing

'Age is mind over matter, if you don't mind, it doesn't matter'
MARK TWAIN

My belief: It's not the aged that feel old, but that they are made to feel their age, by agencies of their making: for example, family, friends, associates or where they worked and have now retired. Its always other peoples' perceptions and judgements that dwarf us, if we do not stand up to them. They attack our vulnerabilities and diminish us. What is needed is 'strength of the spirit' to shield us from being intimidated. What is needed is a strong sense of self with a consistent centre to withdraw into and get restored. *A rendezvous with the soul*!

Relationship with Time

"The years teach us much, which the days never know."

RALPH WALDO EMERSON

Our relationship with time past, present and future is a constant one. It is akin to our relationship with the soul. Both are gifts we are yet to recognize. So, we spend them carelessly, 'kill time' and not take cognizance of these precious gifts, till it is late, and the steam engine of life blows its whistle. Then we know we must go, taking our dreams and best intentions. We do not know where we are going.

We need to turn to our souls and let them steer us. When we say time is running, it is we who are running.

The question is: 'From who are we running and to who are we running?'
'From where to where are we running?' 'Do we know? Do we care?'

The Wisdom Tree

It is the summer of 1990. The Diocese of Varanasi invites me to run a laboratory in teaching English: 'Reading, Writing, Conversation and Grammar'. I am delighted. Indian Airlines sponsors my ticket. I stay with the priests and sisters, who have come to attend the workshop from all over the country.

Everyone is engaged and beaming. I feel success in their reaching out to me, acknowledgement, validation, and more. It is the last day of a very successful workshop. Father Thomas has arranged a visit to 'Sarnath', the place where Buddha received enlightenment. There are a lot of stupas and edicts bearing his teachings. These were constructed by King Ashoka who became a Buddhist after winning the Kalinga war and seeing the bloodshed. He had entire India, Pakistan, Burma, Sri Lanka and Tibet and Nepal in his empire, but he did not feel happy.

Walking on the battlefield, he saw blood and bones, warriors who left behind their families. King Ashoka's heart saddened as he said:

'True victory lay over the hearts of people and not over their lands or possessions'.

He patronised Buddhism and sent his ambassadors far and wide to spread Buddha's words of non-violence and peace. These were inscribed on the stupas in the language of the people, 'pali'.

I was at that place watching the edicts with Fr. Thomas. It was a hot day in May. We had walked a considerable distance. Tired, I sat under an old tree. The roots of this tree went into earth and came out and went in again and came out as another tree. This multiplicity of hanging roots, leafy and shady branches mesmerized me. I became curious about the age of the tree. I don't know how long we sat there, as time seemed to have paused. I was not feeling hot or tired anymore. Neither my senses nor my mind were engaged. I was meditating on the tree, its spirit, its energy. This was a *soulful connection.*

Fr. Thomas said, 'we must go now to the temple of Buddha'. It was getting late and the temple would close for the day. It was a must see, as it had frescoes painted on the walls depicting his renunciation, the eightfold path and the four noble truths.

I was amazed to see the art work dating back in history. Buddha had preached there at that very space in the temple. There was silence, a few people walked about quietly. The Buddhist priest who was showing us around, pointed to the same old tree I sat under. My curiosity awakened. 'Yes, that tree', 'I want to know more about it', I said.

'That is the Bodhi tree, under which Buddha received enlightenment'.

He had fasted and meditated for several days before he came to the realization of the four noble truths and

The Wisdom Tree

found the eightfold path to achieve 'nirvana' or freedom from sorrow. Another awakening of the soul!

Was it a coincidence, or had the spirit of the tree beckoned me to take shelter and thus connect with me? Was it a soulful reaching out by the tree or an unidentified thirst in me?

The moment became surreal. A little while ago, I was sitting under that tree and wondering how old it was. As if the tree was speaking to me or aware of my question, it brought about a vibration of peace and harmony. Was the 'Buddha mind' still there, some remnant of his consciousness that lingered thousands of years later?

It was an experience that cannot be put into words.

On the way back, I saw at the banks of the Ganges, bodies being cremated, just what Buddha had seen before he left the palace gates, I saw sick and old people, just what Buddha saw and asked his friends who they were.

His insulated life in the palace was not conscious of the truths of sickness, age and death. When he did become conscious, he saw the futility of living a life of illusion. His soul yearned to find meaning in life. He reached out to an ignorant humanity 'caught in the act of getting and spending energy and time in insubstantial ways.'

Perhaps Buddha's *'eightfold path'* was the message of the Bodhi Tree: **'***Awakening of one's consciousness, Recognition and Realization of the self'*.

Being open to experience, I had made a connection. I remember the tree and its vibrations. Just remembering them brings peace and shade to the present moment.

Trees symbolize 'wisdom'.
I wonder: 'Did Buddha choose the tree or did the tree choose Buddha?'
'Had I chosen the tree or had the tree called me?'

My relationship with trees has altered since that experience. I look up to them and try to feel their vibrations. I find solace in them, when weary or at a loose end.

"*Buddham, Sharnam, gachami*", meaning 'come to the Buddha.' Buddha means the wise one. These words come to mind. When I see trees felled, it saddens me. 'I think we should revere trees, not fell them without cause', I say to the class.

Someone pipes in: 'One way to avoid unnecessary felling is to use paper efficiently'.

I understand that trees are more than their product. They are spirited and wise, our mentors and benefactors. This is our takeaway for the day.

Science of Wisdom

MADAME BLAVATSKY, THE THEOSOPHIST

'Before the soul can stand in the presence of the 'Masters' its feet must be washed in the blood of the heart.'

ANNIE BESANT

Love is the key to soul realization. Recognizing love in its true essence when we encounter it, is the way. Learning from it, is the means to evolution and Grace.

The blood covenant is the sacrifice made in love.

Theosophy or 'the science of wisdom', takes us to a life of clairvoyance.

'The Voice of Silence' is the bible of the Theosophists. It is essential in reaching out to this world and to the astral world. Trying to understand the masters and their works I draw conclusions.

Many people wonder why sorrow comes to them and struggles are a part of their lives. They envy those who they think are bereft of these. The truth is that no one is bereft of sorrow or struggle. Everyone must deal with it, to manage it.

> *Struggle is the effort to squeeze through the narrow gate of evolution experientially.*
> *What then is the prime function of emotional, mental, physical, social, cultural and spiritual struggles?*

At each level, there is a 'Truth' being learnt, a realization experienced down the road. It is not an armchair exercise. Hence, one must go through the fire to learn about its heat and one's forbearance and strength to come out of it. It's a stress test for the heart, testing forbearance. Keep running on the tread mill till one pants.

The light is not necessarily at the end of the tunnel. Sometimes it is along the way. Those few delightful 'aha' moments of soulful awakening! They can be brought about by the soul, the mind or the body. Let's look for them.

Soul to me is the love seat. From here I perceive the world. When there are heartbreaks, I put them down as sacrifices made, in order to learn life's lessons, to graduate soulful learning and assimilate all that comes my way with a loving spirit.

Forgiving is a part of it, recognizing my humaneness is another part of it. Being humbled by another's achievement and growth exalts not diminishes me. To grow in love is to accept the other and make space for expression, for folly, for love. If this is not love, I wonder what is?

The Maze

Narrow is the gate through which we must enter. The path we are destined to walk is strewn with challenges. Often, we make mistakes and misperceive our tribulations. We are stymied by ingratitude. It stares at us like a slap in the face. We then wonder: Is this the result of having sacrificed for those who turn their backs on us?

If we had only realized that these are the nets from which **'The Fisherman'** would take what is valuable, lasting, and has potential. He will then ask some other fishermen to drop their nets and follow him. Who will he ask and who will follow him is the question?

Are we preparing ourselves for the great astral journey ahead, or are we caught up in the blizzard of self aggrandisement?

The mist clears. I can see with clairvoyance. I feel a sense of harmony, no doubt at all, a peace that surpasses the trivial and temporary. It is exhilarating!

We travellers are unaware where the path leads, we begin to doubt and ask: "Why me?". Sometimes our perceptions blind us to reality. At other times we are caught in a swirl of material dust, 'getting and spending, we lay waste our powers', as Wordsworth would say. It is this quagmire I must get out of. It is this blinded lane of self-creation that is a dead end. Yet, we are in the maze.

Are we finding our way out of the maze, or getting more entangled as time comes closer to end the journey?

This is the question we must ask ourselves perpetually at each rung of the ladder.

The Bird flies home

when the situation gets impossible,
there is spiritual surgence
of truths not felt before
in their clairvoyance
i distinguish
fear from faith
friend from foe
creation from destruction
and illusion from reality

this strengthens the weak branch
with its roots in heavens

what falls apart is the crust
of the superficial layers
that held one captive

the parochial lens loses
its power to blindfold
emerging realities

truths both
known and unknown
surface like creatures
from another world
coming up for oxygen

'yes' becomes more powerful than 'no'
'possibility thinking' more than 'perception'

amidst the crowds
among the critics
lost friends and
those who turned away
when the waters got rough

i stand 'alone'
but not 'lonely'
'tired' but not 'weary'
my heart is heavy
but not from
what happens to those who care

but from what is possible
but does not materialize
lost potential
despirited beings

running the marathon with fearful limbs
easily influenced by theories
that speak the language of
another's experience
and can never be generalized

false perception
with its roots in the ego

when the snow melts
it is water and it is fluid

The Bird flies home

when ego melts
and opinions give way
to another way of seeing
there is understanding

served on the experiential tray
after much is spilled and lost

in the water that exceeds the mass
we sail our paper boats to unknown shores
elated and debating with our fellow beings
whose is better?

like children at play, we cry out
immersed in the making and in the taking
we lose sense of omnipotent time

illuminating dark corners of confusion
with this celestial knowledge
the Spirit surges potions
disengages sorrow from delight

and the bird flies home !

ACKNOWLEDGEMENTS

I acknowledge the presence and contribution of innumerable souls who helped stir my thoughts and enabled me to pen them down at various stages in my life, to share them with you.

I am grateful to Brian Beal for his validation and appreciation of my weekly reflections that brought about this printed version. You made this possible Brian!

Avinash Pasricha you did it again! Your pictures augment my writing as always.

Philip, I thank you for writing the foreword to 'Cultural Awakenings' and for being the mentor I can turn to at all times on this journey. It means a lot to me.

I thank Hansib Publications for their effort in bringing the trilogy to a close.

I am appreciative of the Symbiosis Law Schools in India and the appreciation of the students and staff of Symbiosis Law Schools all over India of my workshops and books.

Thank you Mallika Sarabhai for arranging readings at the British Council Library.

I thank Soli Sorabjee and Dr. Kavita Sharma for their public readings of my works at the I.I.C.

I thank the august thinker, philosopher and writer Dr. Karan Singh for his appreciation of my writings. I appreciate 'Michael Dias and Associates' Law firm for protecting my intellectual assets. I am grateful to Y.M.C.A. Geneva Park for arranging readings on the banks of Lake Couchiching, and to all those who came to the microphone to read and to buy 'Signature Cultures,' 'Cultural Conundrums' and now 'Cultural Awakenings.'